Favourite Yorkshire Recipes

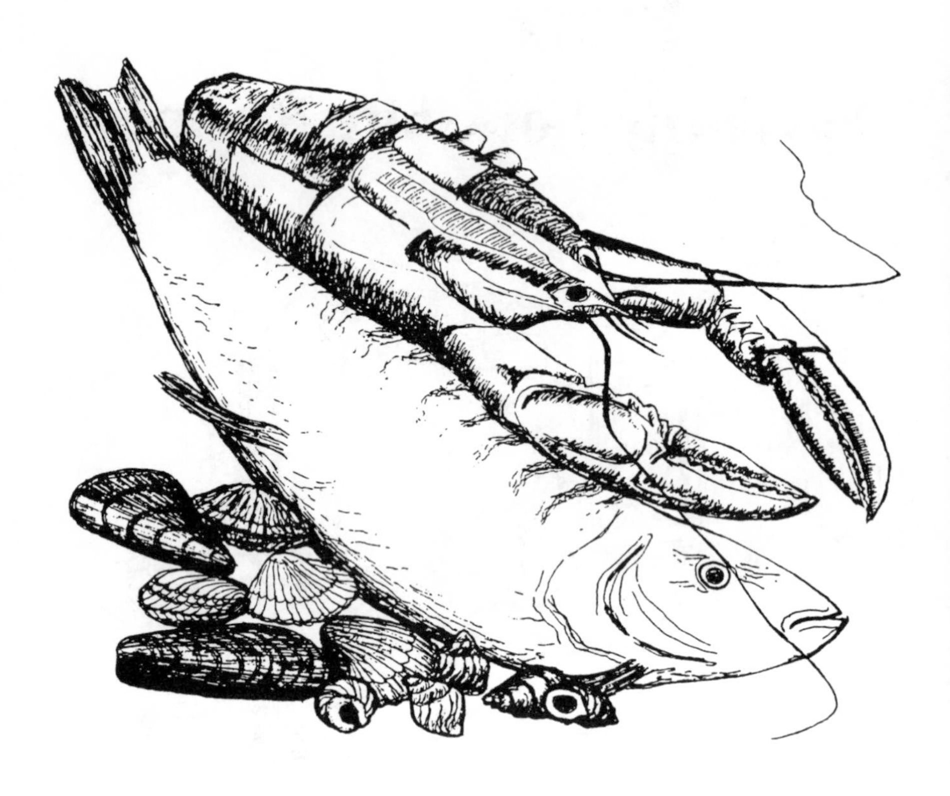

Favourite Yorkshire Recipes

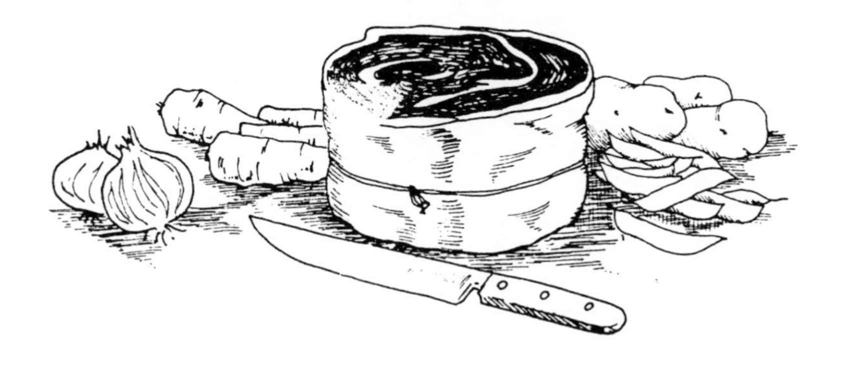

Dalesman Books 1990

The Dalesman Publishing Company Ltd.
Clapham, via Lancaster, LA2 8EB.

First published 1990

ISBN: 1 85568 009 2

Printed in Great Britain by
Peter Fretwell & Sons Ltd., Goulbourne Street, Keighley, West Yorkshire BD21 1PZ.

Contents

Oven Settings

Some of the recipes in this book use traditional descriptions for oven settings. The conversion factors for electric and gas ovens are as follows:-

	Electric	Gas
Very Slow	250	1
Slow	300	2
Moderate	350	4
Hot (or quick)	400	6
Very Hot	475	8

Introduction

YORKSHIRE has long been noted for providing good, wholesome fare. Anyone who leaves a Yorkshire table without having satisfied the inner man would surely have no-one to blame but himself!

To help us compile these mouth-watering menus, Yorkshire personalities and Dalesman readers have provided us with some of their own tried and tasted recipes for complete meals. Our grateful thanks must go to all those whose contributions have been included.

No Yorkshire recipe book would be complete without the old traditional favourites and for these, we must thank our predecessors for their culinary skills – and hearty appetites.

Acknowledgements

Susan Brookes presents "Brookes Cooks" on the Granada TV programme "This Morning". David Watson is Head Chef at Hanni and Michael Gill's nationally renowned Pool Court Restaurant with Rooms, at Pool-in-Wharfedale near Leeds.

Starters

STARTERS

Lettuce Soup

1 oz butter
1 medium-sized onion
1 (½ lb) large potato
1½ pints chicken stock
1 large head of lettuce or 2-3 smaller ones
Salt, pepper

Melt the butter in a large pan. Add finely chopped onions. Cover and fry gently for about five minutes. Peel and dice the potatoes and add to pan. Toss them in onion-flavoured butter and cook for a few minutes. Add the stock. Bring to the boil, then simmer for about 15 minutes.

Coarsely shred washed lettuce leaves. Add lettuce to pan. Bring to the boil and draw pan off heat. Do not cook the lettuce. Put all into an electric blender. Season. Return to pan to re-heat for serving hot. Can be served cold.

— Marie Hartley & Joan Ingilby

Celeriac, Parsnip and Chestnut Soup

Celeriac and parsnips: equal quantities of each after peeling and slicing (approx. 8 oz each).
1 onion
2 sticks celery
1 medium leek
2-3 pints chicken stock
salt and pepper
chestnuts for garnish (chopped)
1 oz butter
pint cream

Roughly chop the onion, celery and leek, then "sweat off" in a saucepan with the butter. Add the celeriac and parsnips and cover with the chicken stock. Cook well - until almost a puree - then pour into a liquidiser; finally, pass the mixture through a sieve.

To finish: Add the cream, season to taste, and garnish with the chestnuts.

If the soup is too thick, add more chicken stock until the consistency you require is achieved).

Serves 6-8.

— David Watson

Carrot and Orange Soup

1 lb carrots
1 small onion or ½ large one, diced
1 pint chicken stock (or pint of water and ½ chicken stock cube)
juice of large orange
½ level teaspoon sugar
milk - about ½ pint off top of the bottle to include the cream
salt and pepper to taste
a little margarine or butter

In a pan gently fry onion in butter or margarine. Top, tail, and chop carrots (but don't peel) and add to pan together with stock. Simmer gently until the carrots are very tender - ½ hour should be plenty then liquidise (if you don't have one push through sieve with a wooden spoon or mash with potato masher). It will be fairly thick at this stage.

Add the juice of the orange, sugar, salt and pepper according to how much you like and the top third of a bottle of milk. Reheat and you will have a thickish soup with a very delicate taste.

To posh it up for guests you could put a blob of cream and/or some chopped parsley on each serving.

— Susan Brookes

Leek and Potato Soup

3 tablespoons butter
3 leeks
4 large potatoes
¾ cup water
1 quart milk
Salt and pepper to taste
Paprika

Melt the butter in a two-quart pot. Wash and chop the leeks and saute them in the butter. Peel and slice the potatoes and add them to the leeks. Add the water; cover.

Cook until both potatoes and leeks are soft enough to put through a sieve. After the mixture has been put through the sieve, add hot milk to it, stirring constantly. Season with salt and pepper.

Serve the soup with a dash of paprika on top of each portion. Makes six servings.

— Jennifer Whitaker

Courgette and lemon soup

2 lbs courgettes, washed and thickly sliced
1 medium potato, peeled and cut into large pieces
2 medium onions, peeled and chopped small
1 large lemon, or two small ones
1¾ pints good chicken stock
salt and white pepper
2 oz butter

Thinly peel the rind from the lemon. Place the courgettes, onions and potato into a large pan in which you have melted the butter, stir the vegetables to coat and cook slowly for about 5 minutes. Pour on half the stock and add the lemon rind. Cover the pan and simmer for 30 minutes. Too long a cooking will spoil the flavour. Blend, then place all through a sieve, add the remainder of the stock and the juice from the lemon, season. Reheat. Stir in a little cream before serving. Serve with warm chunks of oatmeal soda bread.

— Barbara Hopkinson

Oatmeal Soda Bread

12 oz plain wholemeal flour
1 oz butter or white vegetable fat
4 oz medium oatmeal
1 level teaspoon salt
¼ teaspoon sugar
2 level teaspoons bicarbonate of soda
about ½ pint milk and water mixed

Grease two six-inch shallow cake tins. Rub the fat into the dry ingredients, add all the liquid at once and stir round with the hand, add a little more milk to make a soft scone-like dough. Lightly shape with the hands adding a few rolled oats to shape into two rounds, place in the prepared tins. Bake at 220° C, 425° F for 25 minutes until well risen and brown. Turn out and cool a little before cutting into chunks. Best eaten the same day.

— Barbara Hopkinson

Tuna & Orange Pate

1 small onion, peeled and very finely chopped
¼ oz margarine
1 tin of tuna (7½ oz) drained and mashed
Finely grated rind of half a small orange
2 tablespoons of Thousand Island dressing
1 tablespoon single cream
Salt and pepper

Gently fry the onion in the margarine until it is soft and translucent, but not brown. Mix it into the tuna along with the grated orange rind, Thousand Island dressing and cream. Season lightly and press into a small bowl. Serve with a little fresh salad and wholemeal bread.

— Hilary Whitbread

Smoked Mackerel Pate

10 oz smoked mackerel
4 oz natural cottage cheese
Juice of ½ lemon
1 heaped teaspoon grainy mustard
1 teaspoon Worcester sauce
A good twist of black pepper
1 tablespoon natural yoghurt
1 tablespoon chopped parsley

Put all ingredients into blender and mix until creamy. Serve with toast or granary bread.

— Anita Hall

Prawn Tartlets

8 oz frozen prawns
12 small slices brown bread
A little butter
3 tablespoons mayonnaise
1 tablespoon chopped fresh herbs - suggest chives or parsley or dill

Using a 3-inch round pastry cutter, cut a circle out of each slice of bread - this will leave you with lots of bits which you can use to make breadcrumbs. Flatten each round of bread slightly with a rolling pin, and lightly butter each one. Butter the 12 indentations of the usual size bun tray (patty tins) and place a buttered round of bread on each one. They will need to be weighted down with baking beans or whatever you use to "bake blind" to make the shape of a little tart case. Bake in a hot oven, gas 7, 220° C, for eight minutes till the shapes have firmed up and begun to go brown and crisp. Tip out the baking beans and put back in the oven for a minute to crisp the centre, then lift on to a wire rack to cool.

Reserve 12 of the thawed prawns for garnish, and put the rest of the prawns in a bowl with the chopped fresh herbs and the mayonnaise. Stir well to coat, then divide this between the bread cases. Finish by topping with the reserved prawns, and a leaf of fresh herb if you have any left over.
Makes 12 tartlets.

— Susan Brookes

Herring Marinade

2 jars pickle herring
2 eating apples
Tablespoon lemon juice
Large carton natural yoghurt
Cucumber
Black pepper

Drain and flake the herring. Place in dish with diced apple. Add lemon juice, black pepper and yoghurt. Leave overnight to marinade. 15 minutes before serving, slice cucumber and cover as a pie-crust. Place back into fridge for 15 minutes to crisp the cucumber. Serve with french bread.
Serves four.

— Veronica Trueman

Melon filled with Prawns

Seafood Sauce
3 tablespoons mayonnaise
1 tablespoon tomato sauce
salt and black pepper
Worcester sauce

Halve melon and scoop out the seeds. Fill each half with prawns and spoon sauce over. Serve with brown bread.

Serves two.

— Ann Foster

Citrus Starter

2 grapefruit
3 oranges
Quarter honeydew or half a Gallia melon
3 tablespoons orange juice
juice of lime
2 oz pine kernels
1 oz flaked almonds

Peel the grapefruit, divide into segments, remove pith. Cut each segment into two. Cut away peel from oranges, slice horizontally. Cut each slice into four. Cut the melon into dice. Mix all prepared fruit together in a bowl and add orange and lime juice. Chill for at least 30 minutes. Before serving lightly toast the pine kernels and almonds and use as garnish.

Serves six.

— Hazel Wheeler

Pears Sublime

2 good sized, fairly ripe fresh pears
4 oz Philadelphia cheese
Dessertspoon lemon juice
12 black grapes

Peel pears, carefully cut in half and remove cores. Fill each half with cream cheese to which you have added lemon juice. Decorate with halved grapes, de-pipped and placed face down on cheese. Serve in individual shallow dishes.

— Irene Megginson

Salade Niçoise

1 lb cooked potatoes
1 lb cooked French beans
Vinaigrette dressing
1 small can anchovy fillets
2 tomatoes (quartered)
12 black olives approx. 1 doz each black and green grapes
lettuce or chicory
chopped parsley

Dice potatoes and slice French beans. Halve grapes and remove pips. Stone olives. Arrange lettuce or chicory in serving dish or bowl. Toss all other ingredients in vinaigrette dressing and arrange on bed of lettuce or chicory. Sprinkle with chopped parsley just before serving.

I like to add small chunks of Greek feta cheese. 3-4 servings.

— Marylyn Webb

Mini Kebabs

4 sausages
4 rashers back bacon
4 pineapple slices

Grill the sausages and bacon and cut into pieces. Cut the pineapple slices into chunks. Thread the bacon, sausage and pineapple on to cocktail sticks and serve.

— Hilary Whitbread

Nettle Pancakes

Make a pancake batter in your favourite way and cook a pile of thin pancakes.

Nettle filling:
Wash young nettles, wearing gloves; do not drain. Cook the nettles quickly, in the water that sticks to them; toss in butter and chop finely with lemon juice and black pepper.

Remove rind from lean bacon, dice and fry until crisp.

Put one pancake in an ovenproof dish, add a layer of nettle filling and top with bacon. Cover with a second pancake and a layer of nettles as before and build up 8 to 10 layers. Sprinkle with grated cheese and cook in a slow oven for 20 minutes. Serve hot in slices.

— Ann Williams

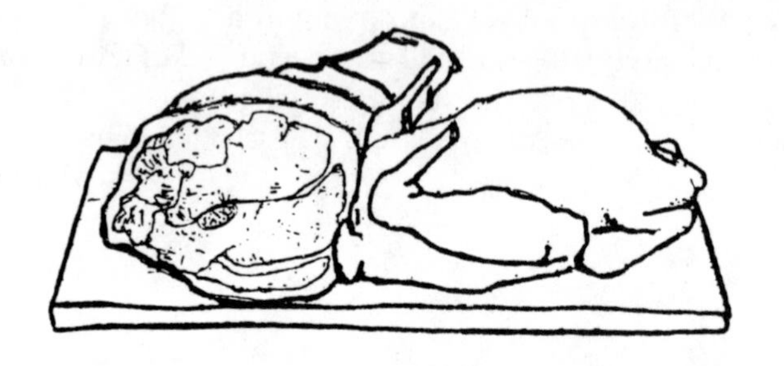

Main Courses

Main Courses

Salmon Steaks in Filo, with Cucumber sauce.

4 fresh salmon steaks about 1 inch thick
2 oz butter
1 glass white wine
1 tablespoon finely chopped dill
1 tablespoon finely chopped parsley
⅔ oz melted butter
Filo or streudal pastry
⅓rd of a large cucumber
½ pint creamy milk
2 tablespoons plain flour
salt and pepper

Cook the salmon in a covered dish with the wine and the butter. Cook until the salmon alters in texture, about 15 minutes. Leave to cool in the liquid, skin and bone the salmon and strain off the liquid to measure ⅓ pint.

Carefully handle the pastry, immediately wrapping and freezing the remainder. Cut (with scissors is easier) three pieces large enough to enclose the salmon steak. Brush each piece with melted butter and place one on top of the other, a salmon steak in the centre, season and add a little chopped dill and parsley. Enclose the salmon by folding the pastry over. Repeat until all the steaks are wrapped.

Place on a lightly greased baking sheet. Brush the top with butter. They may remain like this for about half an hour if you wish, until you are ready to cook them. Bake in a medium oven for 20 to 25 minutes, until the pastry is brown and crisp. Reg. 6. 400° F, 200° C.

Whilst they are baking, slice the washed cucumber and place in a blender with the flour, ½ pint creamy milk, butter and strained liquid from the fish. Blend until smooth. Turn into a small pan. Use a balloon whisk, cook and whisk gently until a thick and smooth sauce is obtained. Season, and a squeeze of lemon can be added, and a little cream. Serve each salmon steak with a little sauce, garnish with parsley and serve with a green salad and steamed new potatoes.

Alternatively you can use two fillets of cooked trout in place of the salmon and add chopped fennel in place of the dill.

— Barbara Hopkinson

Halibut Steaks in Shrimp Sauce

4 halibut steaks
White sauce
Small tin shrimps (or equivalent in frozen ones)

Wash and dry fish, add a little salt and pepper. Wrap in foil with generous knob of butter. Place in ovenproof dish and bake in moderate oven till tender. Meanwhile, make up a pint of milk into sauce with seasoned flour and 1 oz butter, using the "Roux" method finally adding the shrimps. Remove cooked steaks carefully from foil and arrange in serving dish - cover with sauce reserving some for guests who may like a little extra. Sprinkle with parsley. Serve with selection of vegetables. This dish can be kept hot in a low oven till taken to the table.

— Irene Megginson

Lobster Thermidor

2 medium lobsters
4 oz mushrooms
8 oz tomatoes
2 oz butter
1 ½ cups of milk
1-2 oz of grated cheese
seasoning
½ tea cup of sherry or white wine
1 oz flour

Fry skinned and sliced tomatoes until very soft. Stir in flour and cook for 3 minutes. Gradually add milk. Bring to the boil and cook until thickened. Season well. Stir in the flaked lobster meat and wine/sherry. Pile into halved lobster shells. Sprinkle with cheese and brown under the grill. Serve hot.

— Veronica Trueman

Piquant Prawns

3 tablespoons vegetable oil
1 medium-sized onion, finely chopped
2 garlic cloves, crushed
14 oz canned peeled tomatoes
2 tablespoons tomato purée
2 tablespoons wine vinegar
¼ teaspoon dried basil
¼ teaspoon cayenne pepper
1 teaspoon prepared mustard
½ teaspoon salt (optional)
1 teaspoon sugar, 1 lb frozen prawns or shrimps, thawed and drained
2 tablespoons stuffed olives, sliced

In a large frying-pan heat the oil over a moderate heat. When the oil is hot, add the onion and garlic and fry them, stirring occasionally, for 5 to 7 minutes or until the onion is soft and translucent but not brown.

Stir in the tomatoes with the can juice, tomato purée, vinegar, basil, cayenne, mustard, salt and sugar and bring the mixture to the boil. Cover the pan, reduce the heat to low and simmer the sauce for 25 minutes.

Add the prawns or shrimps, and stir them into the sauce. Increase the heat to moderate and bring the mixture to the boil again. Cover the pan, reduce the heat to low and simmer for a further 10 minutes. Taste the sauce and add more pepper or sugar if necessary.

Remove the pan from the heat. Spoon the mixture into a heated serving dish. Scatter over the olives and serve in a ring of boiled rice.

Serves 4 to 6.

— Marylyn Webb

Haddock Barrie

4 fresh haddock fillets (each approx. 6 oz)
12 peeled prawns
Seasoned flour
2 oz butter
1 oz plain flour
½ pint milk
2 oz cheddar cheese
1 small onion
Salt and cayenne pepper
3 fluid oz double cream

Wash the fillets thoroughly and pat them dry on kitchen towel. Coat each fillet lightly with seasoned flour. Use half the butter to grease a shallow flameproof dish and arrange the fillets in a single layer in this. Melt the remaining butter in a small pan, stir in the flour, cook for a few minutes, then gradually add the milk to make a white sauce. Grate the cheese and blend into the sauce, together with the peeled and finely chopped onion, add also the prawns. Season with salt and cayenne pepper and stir in the cream.

Pour the sauce over the fish and bake in the centre of an oven, pre-heated to 400°F (Gas 6) for 30 minutes. If it has not browned by this time put the dish under a hot grill for a few minutes.

Serve the fillets at once; plain boiled rice or new potatoes and a green vegetable, such as spinach, go well with this dish.

Serves 4.

— Ann Foster

Sesame Chicken

4 large or 8 small chicken thighs
2 level tablespoons sesame seeds

Marinade:
8 tablespoons dark soy sauce
2 tablespoons orange marmalade
1-inch fresh ginger, grated, or ½ teaspoon ground ginger
1 tablespoon sesame oil
2 cloves garlic, peeled & crushed

Place all marinade ingredients in a deep bowl. Skin chicken thighs and put into marinade, ensuring marinade covers chicken. Leave for at least 2 hours turning at least once.

Put chicken on a rack over a baking tray. Sprinkle with sesame seeds and cook at 220°C/425°F/Gas 7 for the first 15 minutes. Baste with any marinade mixture which drips into base of tray. Turn oven down to 190°C/375°F/Gas 5 for a further 15-30 minutes. When chicken joints thoroughly cooked the chicken can be served hot or cold.

Serves 4.

Susan Brookes

Chicken Marengo

3½ lb oven-ready chicken
1 oz lard
Salt
8 oz mushrooms, stalked and sliced
1 oz butter

Sauce:
1½ oz butter
2 sticks celery, chopped
1 small carrot, peeled and chopped
2 medium onions, peeled and chopped
1 rasher of bacon, rinded and diced
1 mushroom, chopped
1 tomato, quartered
Sprig of parsley
Blade of mace
Bay leaf
Salt and freshly ground pepper
1½ oz flour
2¼ oz can concentrated tomato paste
1 pint chicken stock
1 tablespoonful sherry

Roast the chicken, heat the lard and pour over the chicken. Season skin with salt.

To make the sauce, heat butter in saucepan. Add celery, carrot, onions, bacon, mushroom, tomato, parsley, mace, bay leaf, salt and pepper. Fry gently, stirring until dark golden brown all over. Add flour and stir well, then add tomato paste.

Slowly add stock, stirring constantly to prevent lumps appearing. Add sherry. Bring to the boil, stirring. Cover and simmer for approx one hour.

Remove flesh from chicken and cut into manageable pieces. Place in a large casserole. Saute mushrooms in butter and add to casserole. Strain sauce over chicken, discard vegetables.

Cover, cook in the oven at 350°F (Mark 4) for ½ hour to heat thoroughly.

Serve with potatoes or rice.

Serves 6.

— Jennifer Whitaker

Pot-Roasted Guinea Fowl

2 x 2 lb guinea fowls
3 oz split green peas
3 oz split yellow peas
8 oz parsnip
8 oz carrot
8 oz swede
8 oz courgette
2 tablespoons vegetable oil
1 pint good quality chicken stock
salt and pepper
chervil

Firstly remove the breasts from the guinea fowls, then the legs and separate the drumsticks from the thighs. Chop the remaining carcass into small pieces and add to the chicken stock - bring to the boil, reduce by half, then pass through a fine sieve.

Cook the split peas in boiling, salted water until just soft, then refresh by dipping immediately into cold water.

Prepare the peeled vegetables, either by cutting into ½ inch strips or "turning" into small barrel shapes.

Season the pieces of guinea fowl and dry in the hot oil until golden brown; remove and drain on kitchen paper.

Lay the guinea fowl legs and thighs in a shallow, oven-proof casserole, add the stock, cover and cook in a medium to hot oven for approximately 10 minutes. Then add the breasts and the vegetables (except the courgettes) and continue simmering for another 10-15 minutes, or until cooked to your taste. Add the split peas and courgettes, bring back to the boil for a couple of minutes, then season to taste.

Arrange attractively on a large plate and sprinkle with a little chopped chervil.

This dish is equally delicious using good quality, corn-fed chickens.

Serves 4.

— David Watson

Pork Oriental

1½ lbs pork fillet
2-3 tablespoons cooking oil
large onion, peeled and sliced
Salt, pepper, chicken stock cube
½ pint water (boiling)
8 oz can pineapple chunks
2 oz plain flour
1 tablespoon vinegar
Soy sauce to taste
Chopped green pepper

Fry onion in oil in casserole. Toss cut meat in bag of seasoned flour, put in with onion. Add water to stock cube, pour over meat and chopped green pepper and vinegar, juice of pineapple, soya sauce to taste. Bring to boil, cover, simmer 1½ hrs. Half an hour before serving add pineapple chunks. Can be made previous day. But do not add pineapple chunks until just before serving.

— Marie Hartley & Joan Ingilby

Harvest Casserole

The fowl

1 pheasant (or any other fowl)
1 carrot
1 stick of celery
1 onion
1 bay leaf
Sprig of thyme
½ pint of water

The vegetables

½ lb potatoes
½ lb carrots
6 sticks of celery
1 cauliflower
2 leeks
1 lb peas or beans

The sauce

2 oz butter
6 oz flour
1 pint of stock
½ pint of milk
Salt/pepper
4 oz grated cheese

First of all boil the pheasant in a pan until tender, and keep the stock, for use in the sauce. Cook the vegetables in a pan. Strip the flesh off the pheasant and put into the casserole with the cooked vegetables and pour the sauce over them. Cook in a moderate oven for ½ hour.

Place cheese on top and brown under the grill when ready to eat.

— **Alex Welch**

Pork in Cider

4 leg steaks
8 oz sliced mushrooms
1 large onion, finely chopped
2 oz butter
1 teaspoon herbs
Salt and pepper
5 fluid oz dry cider
4 oz grated cheddar cheese
4 tablespoon toasted breadcrumbs
Parsley, for garnish

Put sliced mushrooms in greased dish. Scatter onions and herbs on top and season. Trim fat off meat and lay on top of vegetables. Pour cider over to come level with meat. Mix cheese and breadcrumbs and put over chops. Dot with butter. Cook 200°C, 400°F, Gas 6 for 45 mins.

— Anita Hall

Venison Casserole

1 lb stewing venison
2 shallots
4 oz lean bacon
4 medium carrots
thyme, black pepper, salt, 1 bayleaf
½ cup red wine
1 small tin champignons
Sour cream
Flour

Cut meat into 1-inch cubes. Cut bacon into strips and cook in oil. Remove bacon, add meat and brown on all sides. Cut carrots and shallots into slices and add to meat. Stir frequently. Fry until shallots turn slightly brown. Season with thyme, salt, pepper and bayleaf. Add wine, turn into casserole dish and cook in a slow oven for about 45 minutes or until meat is tender. Drain champignons, add to casserole with bacon 5 minutes before serving. Mix cream and flour and thicken the boiling liquid. Serve with jacket potatoes and tossed green salad.

— Ann Williams

Stilton and Walnut Pie with Celery, Apple and Watercress

Wash the celery and watercress, cut celery into half sticks, but take the apples whole as they discolour so quickly. Take the pie whole and give each person a slice of pie and some pieces of the celery, apple and watercress to eat with it. The amounts for the pie give a generous slice for 8 people, but it keeps well for several days in the fridge.

Pie Recipe
12 oz flour
6 oz butter or marg
2 eggs or 3 if you egg glaze
12 oz cream cheese
Small bunch parsley
6 oz Stilton cheese with rind removed
6 oz chopped walnuts
Small onion
Salt and pepper
A little oil for frying

Make the pastry by rubbing the butter into the flour - you may have a machine that will do this. Add just enough cold water to bind, then leave the pastry to chill in the fridge, covered, while you prepare the filling. Beat 2 eggs together, peel and finely chop the onion and fry the onion gently in a little oil till just softened. Chop the parsley and mix eggs, cream cheese and parsley together, beating until smooth - this can be done in a food processor. Add the fried onion, chopped walnuts and grated or crumbled Stilton. Season to taste - remember Stilton is a very salty cheese, you may need only pepper and a very little salt.

Grease or line a 9-inch round deepish pie dish or loose-bottomed quiche baking tin. Roll out half the pastry and use to line the base and side, trimming to fit. Spread the cheesy filling on this, smoothing level, then roll out the rest of the pastry to make a lid. Cover the pie, sealing edges with a little water if you wish and use pastry trimmings to make little leaf shapes to decorate the top of the pie. These can be fixed in place with a little beaten egg and you can brush the top of the pie with the rest of the beaten egg to give an attractive glazed finish.

Bake for 45 minutes at Gas 5, 190°C and allow to cool before lifting out of the tin.

— Susan Brookes

All-in-one Shepherd's Pie

1 lb minced beef
2 onions, peeled and chopped
½ oz plain flour
½ pint beef stock
Salt and pepper
Few drops of tabasco sauce
8 oz mushrooms, sliced
1 lb cooked potato
1 lb cooked carrot
2 oz margarine
Salt and pepper

Quickly brown the mince in a pan. Lift the meat out of pan, drain well and put to one side. Gently fry the onion in the fat that has come out of the meat, until it is soft and translucent, but not brown. Add the flour and cook for 2-3 minutes. Stir in the stock. Bring to the boil, stirring continuously and season lightly. Add the tabasco sauce, mince and mushrooms. Cover and simmer gently for 10 minutes. Pour into 4 small ovenproof dishes.

Mash the potato, carrot and margarine together and season lightly. Divide into 4 equal portions and spread over each dish. Cook at 375°F, Gas 5, for 45 minutes.

— Hilary Whitbread

Chinese Pork Salad

1 lb pork fillet, cut into narrow strips and fried in a little corn oil until cooked and nicely browned
1 small onion, peeled and very finely chopped
1 green pepper, seeded and chopped
4 oz mushrooms, washed and sliced
8 ozs cooked long-grain rice, rinsed and drained
1 tablespoon white wine vinegar
1 tablespoon Soy sauce
Salt and pepper

Stir everything together and serve seasoned with Soy sauce.

— Hilary Whitbread

Corn and Asparagus Flan

8 oz shortcrust pastry made with wholewheat flour
1 7-oz can sweetcorn, drained
1 5-oz can asparagus tips, drained
1 small onion, chopped
3 ounces Cheddar cheese, grated
2 large eggs, beaten
½ pint milk
pinch of salt
Freshly ground black pepper

Roll out pastry, line an 8-inch flan tin, or fireproof dish. Bake "blind" for about 10 minutes, or until firm.

Mix corn, asparagus, onion, cheese, eggs and milk together. Add salt and pepper to taste, pout into prepared flan case. Gas Mark 5 until set. Serve hot with vegetables of your choice, or cold with salad or cooked beetroot.

— Hazel Wheeler

Sweets

Sweets

Frozen Meringue Pudding with raspberry coulis

4 to 5 oz meringue shells or rings
10 oz double cream
2 tablespoons Kirsch or Grand Marnier
6 oz raspberries
1½ oz icing sugar, sieved
2 tablespoons port or red wine

Line the base of a 2 pint basin with non-stick paper and very lightly oil the sides only.

Crumble the meringue into pieces about the size of a new 5p. Whip the cream until half whipped, until the whisk leaves a trail. Whip in the Kirsch. Fold in the meringue. Spoon into the basin, cover and freeze.

To make the coulis, press the raspberries through a sieve stir in the icing sugar and the port, brandy or whatever. Thin a little more if necessary. Turn the pudding out on to a serving dish and leave for about 1 hour until it is frozen but not hard. Serve in portions with a little of the coulis, decorate with ratafias and a mint leaf.

— Barbara Hopkinson

Queen of Puddings

½ pint milk
1 oz butter
½ pint fresh bread crumbs
1 egg
2 oz sugar
Grated rind of lemon
Jam

Boil half pint of milk with 1 oz butter and pour over half a pint of bread crumbs. Let it soak for a few minutes, then add the yolk of an egg. Pour into a pie dish and bake until set. Take out of oven, spread with jam (preferably home-made raspberry jam) beat the white of egg stiff, spread over top, sprinkle with sugar and bake pale brown in oven. Serve with cream.

— Marie Hartley & Joan Ingilby

Quick Bread and Butter Pudding

8 slices left over bread and butter
Sultanas
2 tablespoons sugar
3 eggs
1 pint milk

Cut bread and butter into cubes and place in a 2 pint pyrex dish. Add a handful of sultanas and the sugar. Beat 3 eggs and mix in the milk. Pour over bread and butter. Sprinkle with nutmeg. Bake in a medium hot oven for 45 minutes or until set.

Serves 4.

— Ann Foster

Gooseberry and Orange Pudding

1 lb gooseberries
1 orange
1 oz butter/margarine
4 oz brown sugar
1 egg
4 oz white breadcrumbs

Simmer gooseberries in ½ pint water with half the sugar. Melt butter in saucepan and grate the orange rind into it. also the squeezed juice. Beat gooseberries to a pulp with a fork, add beaten egg and tip in butter, rind and juice. Mix.

Butter a fireproof dish and mix the rest of the sugar with the breadcrumbs. Press in half of these to line the base and sides. Spoon in gooseberry mixture and sprinkle rest of breadcrumbs on top. Cover with foil and bake 350°F for 1 hour. Remove foil for last ten minutes to brown.

Serve hot or cold.

— Felicity Manning

Summer Pudding

1 teaspoon of oil
2 lbs raspberries, hulled
4 oz castor sugar
4 fl oz milk
8 slices stale white bread, crusts removed
10 fl or double cream or natural fromage frais

Using the teaspoon of oil, grease a deep pie dish or pudding basin.

Place the raspberries in a large mixing bowl and sprinkle over the sugar. Set aside. Using a teaspoon, sprinkle a little of the milk over each slice of bread to moisten it.

Line the dish or basin with two-thirds of the bread slices, overlapping the edges slightly. Pour the raspberries into the dish or basin and arrange the remaining bread slices on top to cover the raspberries completely.

Place a sheet of greaseproof or waxed paper on top of the dish or basin and put a plate, which is slightly smaller in diameter than the dish or basin, on top.

Place a heavy weight on the plate and put the pudding in the refrigerator to chill for at least 8 hours or overnight.

Remove the pudding from the refrigerator and lift off the weight and the plate. Remove and discard the greaseproof or waxed paper. Invert a serving plate over the top of the dish or basin and, holding the two firmly together, reverse them giving them a sharp shake. The pudding should slide out easily.

Serve with whipped cream, or fromage frais. Blackberries and blackcurrants are also suitable fruit for Summer Pudding.

— Marylyn Webb

Ginger Pudding

8 oz self-raising flour
Large pinch of salt
Round teaspoon of ground ginger
2 oz margarine
2 tablespoons sugar
2 tablespoons treacle
3 tablespoons milk

Mix flour, salt and ginger. Rub in margarine. Add other ingredients and mix well. Put into greased basin and steam for 2-3 hours (or microwave according to instructions). Pour over heated treacle and serve.

— Veronica Trueman

Spiff Chocolate Pudding

8 oz self raising flour
1 oz cocoa
¾ pint milk
5 oz vegetable suet
6 oz brown sugar
4 oz raisins
1 flat teaspoon bicarbonate of soda

Grease a three pint basin and decorate the sides and bottom with raisins, keeping half of them to put into the mixture. Mix all dry ingredients together. Stir in the milk. It makes a moist mixture. Boil for at least 2 hours, the longer the better.

— Felicity Manning

Chocolate Cheesecake

4 oz butter
8 oz digestive biscuits
1 teaspoon cinnamon

Melt butter and add crunched biscuits and cinnamon. Press into 8 oz flan dish.

4 oz dark chocolate
8 oz cottage cheese
2 oz sugar
2 eggs, separated
1 tablespoon gelatine into 2 tablespoons cold water
1 tablespoon rum
¼ pint whipped cream

Blend cheese, sugar and egg yolks. Add melted chocolate and gelatine. Fold in whipped cream and whipped egg whites. Pour over base and pout into fridge till set. (Will freeze).

— Anita Hall

Simply Chocolate

4 oz breadcrumbs, white or brown
pint cream (either whipping, or mixture of double and single)
4 oz demerara sugar
1 tablespoon coffee powder (Nescafe will do if made finer in grinder)
1 tablespoon drinking chocolate or cocoa
A little rum (optional)

Mix dry ingredients. Whip cream adding rum, if liked. Put alternate layers of crumb mixture and cream in glass dish, and leave in fridge overnight. Decorate with chopped nuts and/or cherries.

— Irene Megginson

Almond Treacle Tart

Rich Almond Pastry

5 oz plain flour
4 oz margarine
3 oz ground almonds
2 oz castor sugar
1 egg

Almond and Treacle Filling

5 tablespoons golden syrup
2 oz wholewheat breadcrumbs
2 oz ground almonds

Rich Almond Pastry: Sieve the flour into a bowl and rub in the margarine. Stir in the ground almonds and sugar, add the beaten egg and mix to a firm dough. Roll out and line a greased 9-inch pie plate, keeping a little pastry for the lattice.

Almond and Treacle Filling: Put the golden syrup into a pan and heat gently to warm through. Stir in the breadcrumbs and ground almonds. Pour over the pie dish. Criss-cross with a pastry lattice. Cook at 375°F, Gas 5 for 25 minutes. Cool on a wire rack.

— Hilary Whitbread

Baked Apples

Take large, even, and unblemished cooking apples (one per person). Core the apples and fill the centre with brown sugar, raisins, or sultanas, and a pinch of cinnamon. Put on a baking tray. Cook in a moderate oven until the flesh is soft.

This recipe is also very successful in the microwave oven.

— Alex Welch

Fresh Fruit Salad

2 dessert apples, peeled and chopped
2 pears, peeled and chopped
2 oranges, segmented and chopped
8 oz seedless grapes, washed
8 oz raspberries

Syrup

½ pint water
2 tablespoons whisky
2 oz granulated sugar

Put the water into a pan, add the sugar and heat gently until the sugar dissolves. Stir in the whisky.

Cream Topping

½ pint double cream
1 oz granulated sugar
1 tablespoon whisky

Whisk the cream, sugar and whisky together until it peaks.

Mix the fruit in a bowl, immediately pour on the syrup and mix well. Leave to stand for a few hours then serve with the cream.

— Hilary Whitbread

Blackberry Fool

Stew fresh or frozen blackberries until tender with sugar to taste and lemon juice. Cool, then fold in natural yogurt. Top with cream and whole blackberries; serve chilled.

— Ann Williams

Glazed Fruits (with honey ice cream)

Although there are several elements to this dish, which makes it rather 'labour intensive', the final result is stunning. A selection of seasonal fruits are topped with a glazed sabayon and served with honey ice cream in a light tuile basket. Serves 4.

Honey Ice Cream

6 egg yolks
2 oz caster sugar
18 fl oz milk
5 oz clear honey
2 fl oz double cream

Whisk together the egg yolks and the sugar.

Boil the milk in saucepan and pour over the egg yolk and sugar mixture. Add the honey and return to the pan, stirring continuously until the mixture has thickened.

Away from the heat stir in the double cream. Leave until cold.

Put the mixture into an ice cream maker and freeze. (If you don't have an ice cream maker, then spoon the mixture into a shallow container and freeze. When it begins to harden around the edges — about 30 minutes — take it out and beat it to get rid of the ice crystals. You will need to do this three or four times to make sure the ice cream is really smooth before letting it freeze.)

Tuille Baskets

2 oz unsalted butter
2 oz caster sugar
2 oz liquid glucose
2 oz plain flour

Put the butter and sugar in a blender and beat. Add the glucose, then blend for one minute. Scrape into a bowl and cover with cling film. Leave to rest in the fridge for 2 hours until it has firmed up.

Roll the mixture in the palm of your hand into little balls and place far apart on an oiled baking tray. Press each ball gently into the tray with the palm of your hand. Cook for 3-5 minutes in a moderate oven 350°F/180°C/Gas Mark 4. The mixture will spray out on the tray. Using a cutter the diameter of your tartlet mould or ramekin cut out circles and return these briefly to the oven to soften up again. Press the tuile into the mould or ramekin and place an identical mould into it — thus ensuring a good basket shape.

Sabayon

4 egg yolks
2 oz caster sugar
½ pint Muscat Beaune de Venise

Place all the ingredients together in a stainless steel bowl.

Whisk the mixture over a pan of boiling water until it reaches the ribbon stage (so it leaves whisk marks in the mixture — this takes about 10 minutes).

Place the sabayon on the fruit, then glaze under a very hot grill.

Fruit

A good selection of bright, tasty fruit to fill 4 plates. Suggested fruits: Orange segments/strawberries/raspberries/blackcurrants/redcurrants/blackberries/plums/peaches/pineapple.

— David Watson

Coffee Butterscotch Cream

2 tablespoons custard powder
¾ pint milk
2 tablespoons water
2 oz margarine
3 level tablespoons brown sugar (not demerara)
2 tablespoons cold strong coffee, made either with coffee, powdered coffee or essence. (I like to use what's left over in the coffee pot after 'elevenses' — Viennese ground coffee is my favourite). Cut up stoned dates or walnuts for decoration, and toasted coconut.

Heat sugar and water in strong small saucepan until a brown caramel is formed. Add margarine, gradually stir in milk. Heat, stirring until the caramel is dissolved in the milk.

Mix custard powder to a cream with the coffee and pour boiling liquid in pan on to the cream. Return mixture to pan, stirring all the time to cook for a few minutes until thick.

Spoon into dishes and decorate as desired.

— Hazel Wheeler

Trifle — the real thing!

Plain sponge cake
6 macaroons
1 oz ratafias
¼ pint cooking sherry
3 tablespoons brandy
½ pint double cream
A little grated lemon rind
1 oz blanched almonds, cut in strips
Raspberry jam
½ pint egg custard, freshly made
Garnish: Crystallised fruits and raspberries

Place sponge cake, macaroons and ratafias in a dish. Mix sherry and brandy and pour over them. Over this put the lemon rind, almonds and layer of jam. When the custard is cool, pour it over the trifle.

When it has cooled and set, spread the whipped double cream over top and garnish with crystallised fruits and raspberries.

— Jennifer Whitaker

FLOUR

Traditional Favourites

Traditional Favourites

Yorkshire Pudding

The typical Yorkshire Pudding is made with milk and water to obtain lightness and crispness, and it is essential that there should be no fat in the mixture. Traditionally, it was served with thick gravy, as an individual course before the main course, but is now usually served with roast beef.

1 egg
4 oz flour
1 teaspoon salt
¼ pint milk
¼ pint water

Break the egg into the flour and salt previously mixed in a basin. Add enough liquid to make a beating consistency. Beat well and leave to stand for half an hour. Heat the oven to 450°F.

For small puddings use 2½in. x 1in. size bun tray and put a knob of fat in each tin. Place the tray in the oven until the fat is smoking hot. In the meantime add the rest of the liquid to make a batter.

Take the tray from the oven and put two tablespoons of the batter in each tin. Bake for fifteen to twenty minutes, or use a dripping tin and bake about thirty minutes, then cut the pudding into portions.

Elder Flower Pancakes (Three Recipes)

Recipe 1.
Make the usual pancake mixture. Get one big flower head for each pancake, shake off the pollen, cut the main stem short but leave just enough on to dip the head into the mixture. Fry the dipped head in the usual way. Add a sprinkling of sugar when cooked. Eat the lot.

Recipe 2.
Half-pint milk
Pinch salt
Plain flour
1 egg

Sieve salt and flour into a basin, make a well in centre. Drop in egg yolk and mix some of the flour in gently with a wooden spoon.

Add half the milk gradually, stirring in the rest of the flour. Beat till smooth and free of bubbles. Add the rest of the milk and stand for an hour. Whisk the egg whites until very stiff and fold in before using.

Gather dry, well-opened elderflowers, hold them by the stem, tap sharply to dislodge dust and insects, then dip in the batter and fry lightly in very hot vegetable oil. Sift with fine sugar and hold by the stem to eat.

Recipe 3.
Make a normal soft batter. Cut the elderflowers off the shrub and wash very thoroughly. Dip the flowers into the batter, flowers first, stalk sticking upwards. Put into hot fat in a frying pan.

As soon as the batter sets slightly, cut off all stalks right down to the flower part, then continue frying as a normal pancake. Before serving, sprinkle with sugar.

Serve hot with a slice of lemon, which helps to bring out the flavour of the elderflowers.

Oatcake or Haverbread

These were originally baked on a backstone and the process was quite elaborate. The ingredients, just oatmeal and milk, were allowed to ferment. This recipe gives similar results.

6 heaped tablespoons fine oatmeal
3 heaped tablespoons flour
2 salt spoons salt
½ pint milk
½ pint water
1 oz yeast

Mix together the dry ingredients, warm milk and water (not hot) and mix well together; crumble in the yeast, and let it stand twenty minutes. Cook in a lard-greased frying pan, turn when brown and cook the other side.

Curds

1 pint milk
3 beaten eggs
1 teaspoon salt

Put all ingredients together in a pan and bring to the boil, stir well. Leave on a sieve or in muslin for about 20 minutes, when it is ready for use.

The whey can be used for making scones.

Curd Tarts or Yorkshire Cheese Cakes

½ lb curds
¼ lb sugar
Grated nutmeg (optional)
1 to 2 eggs, well beaten
2 oz currants
½ lb short crust pastry

Line a pie plate with the pastry. Mix the curds, sugar, currants and beaten eggs and pour into the lined pie plate. Sprinkle with nutmeg if liked.

Bake about twenty minutes in a moderately hot oven.

Turf Cakes

These were originally baked on a griddle over a turf fire.

8 oz self-raising flour
4 oz lard
3 oz sugar
2 oz currants
1 oz sultanas
Pinch salt
Water or beaten egg

Rub the lard into the flour and add the rest of the dry ingredients. Mix to a fairly soft dough with a little water or, to make extra good, use a little well-beaten egg. Roll out to about half an inch thickness and cut into rounds.

Bake on a greased tin in a hot oven for ten to fifteen minutes, or until nicely brown.

Pancakes

Pancakes are a very old delicacy, and the custom of eating them on Shrove Tuesday is steeped in history, rites and rituals.

The first "pancake" was probably eaten in ancient Rome! Small flat cakes made with wheaten flour were the most important item served at the great Roman feast called the Feast of the Ovens. This feast was held in the second month of the year, a time when our Shrove Tuesday generally falls, and it seems likely that our pancakes stem from these pagan confections.

Later, when Lent was conscientiously regarded in this country, Shrove Tuesday was the day when the good housewife made sure that all the butter and fat was eaten up before the fast began. This was the day she treated her family to fried pancakes!

In Yorkshire, the first pancake was always thrown to the fowls, and the number of chickens which gathered round to eat the delicacy was taken to indicate the years the cook would have to wait before marrying.

Light Pancake Batter:

4 oz flour—plain
1 egg
Large pinch of salt
½ pint cold milk

Sift flour and salt into a large bowl. Drop in whole egg, then gradually add half the milk stirring in flour from sides of bowl using a wooden spoon. Beat well until mixture is smooth. Gently stir in rest of milk. Use as required. Makes 9 to 10 thin pancakes if cooked in a 9 inch pan.

For extra soft, rich pancakes, add 1 tablespoon olive oil or cooking oil to the batter at the same time as the egg.

For sweet pancakes, sift 1 level tablespoon caster or icing sugar into the bowl with the flour.

Cooking Pancakes

Using a bristle brush or piece of paper, very lightly grease prepared pan with cooking oil or melted lard, and heat till a faint haze just appears. Pour or wipe off any surplus oil or fat. Pour in 2 or 3 tablespoons batter mixture, and quickly tilt pan in all directions until base is completely covered. Cook until underside of pancake is golden, then gently turn over, using a fish slice or broad-bladed palette knife. Turn out, sprinkle with sugar, and roll up the pancake.

N.B.—Avoid using excess oil or fat when making pancakes, as this causes them to stick and break up.

Mincemeat (1)

Take golden pippins pared 2 lb
2 lb well shredded good beef suet
2 lb raisins chopped and stoned
and 2 lb currants to it.

Half ounce cinnamon well-beat
of sugar ¾ of a pound,
And 1 green lemon peel sliced neat
So that it can't with ease be found.

Add sack or brandy glasses three
And 1 large Seville orange squeeze,
Of sweetmeats a small quantity,
And you'll the nicest palate please.

(for sweetmeats use candied peel)

Mincemeat (2)

1 lb finely chopped or shredded suet
1½ lb raisins
1 lb castor sugar
4 oz finely minced blanched almonds
½ level teaspoon grated nutmeg
1 lb currants
1 lb sultanas
1 lb firm cooking apples
4-8 oz finely minced candied peel
¼ level teaspoon mixed spice
½ lemon
6 tablespoons brandy or rum

Having washed and dried fruit, cut raisins into quarters, roughly chop sultanas, leave the currants whole. Peel, core and chop apples.

Mix all ingredients together with brandy, strained juice, and grated rind of lemon. Put into a large wide-mouthed jar. Place a piece of greaseproof paper, cut to fit and dipped in brandy directly on top of mincemeat. Seal jar with two or three thicknesses of greaseproof paper, store in a very cool, dry place.

Plum Pudding

1 lb flour
½ lb suet
6 eggs
1 carrot (grated)
2 slices bread (made into crumbs)
¼ lb mixed peel
¼ nutmeg (grated)
Pinch of all spice
1 teaspoon salt
2 tablespoons treacle
A little milk to mix
10 oz sugar
½ lb raisins
½ lb currants
½ lb sultanas

Mix all ingredients well. Put in greased basins and steam five to six hours.

Hot Cross Buns (usually made for Good Friday)

1 lb flour
Pinch salt
¾ oz yeast
2 tablespoons sugar
2 oz margarine
2 oz currants
1 level teaspoon cinnamon
1 level teaspoon mixed spice
1 egg
About ½ pint milk

Sieve flour with salt and spices, rub in fat and add currants. Cream the yeast with a little sugar, add a little warm milk and pour in centre of flour, sprinkle lightly over with flour and leave for ten minutes. Mix to a stiff dough with the beaten egg, adding a little milk if required.

Allow to rise until the mixture doubles itself in size, divide into twelve portions, mould into small buns, mark with a cross and place on a greased and floured tin. Allow to rise until half as large again. Bake in a hot oven about eight minutes. Melt a little sugar in a tablespoon of milk and brush over the buns when baked.

Tansy Pudding

2 oz white breadcrumbs
1 oz sugar
½ oz butter
2 eggs
½ pint milk
1 dessertspoon finely chopped tansy leaves

Boil the milk and pour over the breadcrumbs; leave for half an hour. Add the well-beaten eggs to the sugar and tansy, mix with the breadcrumbs and milk, add the butter and bake in a pie dish in a moderate oven until set. Eat cold with cream.

Richmond Maids of Honour

The maid of honour tart is reputed to date back to Tudor England. The story has it that in the early happy days of the marriage of Henry VIII and Anne Boleyn the royal party went for a day's hunting to Richmond. Anne and her maids of honour were served with a particular kind of cheesecake. They found these little tarts so delicious that Anne Boleyn invited her husband to try one, too. When he asked what the tarts were called no one could tell him. So the king declared that they should be called Maids of Honour.

Although these little tarts have such a romantic origin, no one agrees about the authentic recipe. For example, some say that puff pastry should be the base — others say short crust.

Pastry:
6 oz plain flour
¼ level teaspoon salt
3 oz butter
½ oz caster sugar
1 egg yolk
1 tablespoon water

Sieve together flour and salt. Rub in butter until mixture resembles fine breadcrumbs. Add sugar and bind together with egg yolk and water to form a stiff dough. Roll out pastry thinly, cut into circles, about 3 inches in diameter, with fluted cutter and line patty tins. Prick base of pastry and chill for a short time if possible.

Filling:
3 oz butter
2 oz caster sugar
4 oz cottage cheese
1 oz chopped blanched almonds
Grated rind of 1 lemon
pinch cinnamon
1 egg and 1 egg white blended together

Cream together butter and sugar until light and fluffy. Add cottage cheese, almonds, lemon rind and cinnamon. Beat in eggs.

Turn mixture into pastry cases and bake in a hot oven for about 25 minutes.

Easter Nest Cake

Sponge Recipe:

4 oz castor sugar
4 large eggs
4 oz plain flour
1 level teaspoon baking powder

Sieve together the flour and baking powder. Separate the yolks from the whites of eggs. Whisk the yolks and sugar till thick, creamy and pale in colour (about 15 minutes), then fold in the stiffly beaten egg whites alternately with the flour.

Turn mixture into two sandwich tins — lightly greased and coated with equal quantities of flour and sugar — and bake in a moderate oven for 30 minutes. When cool, remove a large circle from the centre of one sponge.

Put the remaining ring on top of the other sponge, sandwiching with chocolate butter cream.

Roughly coat the cake all over with the rest of the butter cream and then fill the centre with marzipan or fondant eggs and stand a chick on the inside edge of the ring.

Chocolate Butter Cream:

4 oz butter or margarine
5 oz icing sugar
2 tablespoons cocoa powder
Few drops vanilla essence

Sieve sugar and cocoa powder. Cream with the butter till light and fluffy then add the vanilla essence.

Marzipan Eggs:

1½ oz ground almonds
3 oz icing sugar (sieved)
a little beaten agg

Mix together the sugar and almonds. Add sufficient egg to bind the mixture into a stiff paste. Shape into eggs. For contrast colour some of the paste pink or green.

To speckle the eggs, dot with gravy browning, using a fine paint brush.

Yorkshire Parkin

½ lb flour
½ medium oatmeal
¼ lb soft brown sugar
½ teaspoon ginger
10 oz treacle
3 oz lard
About ¼ pint milk
1 teaspoon bi-carb. soda

Mix together the flour, oatmeal and ginger, melt the sugar, lard and treacle and add a little of the milk. Put this mixture into the flour, etc., and mix to a stiff batter. Add the bi-carbonate of soda dissolved in the rest of the milk.

Mix quickly, pour into a shallow tin 11in x 9in x 2in and bake for about one hour or until firm at 325°F, Gas Mark 2.

Pepper Cake

1½ lb flour
½ lb soft brown sugar
1 teaspoon pearl ash (or bi-carb. soda) melted in little milk
1 oz powdered cloves
1½ lb treacle (not syrup)
½ lb butter
4 well-beaten eggs

Mix all the dry ingredients, rub in the fat, add the pearl ash in milk, the treacle and well-beaten eggs and mix throughly.

Bake in a greased or lined tin in a moderate oven for one and a half to two hours.

Christmas Star Pie

This recipe has extra apples added to the mincemeat and is lighter than the usual mincemeat mixture.

8 oz plain flour
Pinch salt
2 oz butter or margarine
2 oz cooking fat
3 to 4 tablespoons cold water to mix

Filling:
8 oz cooking apples, peeled and finely grated
6 rounded tablespoons mincemeat

Sift flour and salt into bowl. Rub in fats till mixture resembles fine breadcrumbs, then mix to stiff paste with cold water. Turn on to lightly-floured board, knead quickly till smooth, then divide in two. Roll out one half into a round and with it line a well-greased nine inch heatproof plate. Fill with layer of grated apples topped with the mincemeat then moisten pastry round edges with cold water.

For decorative lid, roll out rest of pastry into a ten inch round and cut out a ring of eight stars, about two inches in from outside edge. Place lid carefully over filling and seal firmly.

Arrange cut-out pastry stars round outer edge, holding them in place with a little cold water. Bake pie towards top of oven at 425°F Gas Mark 7 for twenty-five minutes then at 355°F Gas Mark 4 for a further twenty minutes. Dust top with icing sugar and serve warm with cream.

Frumenty

Fifty years ago in the North-East of England, particularly in County Durham and in the Yorkshire dales, a dish of Frumenty was as much a part of Christmas Eve as hanging up stockings is today, and much more so than the still new-fangled Christmas tree was then in those isolated parts. While the children sat round the fire before going to bed, Father would bring in the Yule Log and Mother would put the finishing touches to the traditional Christmas Eve supper — a dish of Frumenty.

Frumenty wheat could always be bought in the local shops around Christmas time. It is the grains of the new wheat, still in the husk.

There are variations on the recipe, but the basis is:

Equal parts of crushed wheat and milk and water; soaked overnight in a stone jar.

It is then cooked for three hours in a slow oven with sugar to sweeten, till the Frumenty is thick and jelly-like.

1 pint milk
1 pint wheat
1 pint water
Sugar to sweeten

The above is a useful amount to make. It can be flavoured with cinnamon or nutmeg, or honey, and currants, too, can be added. Stir these in just before serving and leave until the currants (if used) are soft.

Frumenty is eaten hot, with cream or milk if preferred.

Elderflow
Wine

List of recipes

Starters

Main Courses

Sweets

Traditional Favourites